ANIMALS UN...

BENGAL TIGER

IN DANGER OF EXTINCTION!

D0346162

700027412974

WORCESTERSHIRE COUNTY COUNCIL

297	
BfS	20 May 2005
J 599.756	£7.99

Richard Spilsbury

Heinemann
LIBRARY

H www.heinemann.co.uk/library
Visit our website to find out more information about **Heinemann Library** books.

To order:
☎ Phone 44 (0) 1865 888066
▤ Send a fax to 44 (0) 1865 314091
▢ Visit the Heinemann Bookshop at www.heinemann.co.uk/library to browse our catalogue and order online.

First published in Great Britain by Heinemann Library, Halley Court, Jordan Hill, Oxford OX2 8EJ, part of Harcourt Education. Heinemann is a registered trademark of Harcourt Education Ltd.

© Harcourt Education Ltd 2004
First published in paperback in 2005
The moral right of the proprietor has been asserted.

All rights reserved. No part of this publication may be reproduced, stored in a retrieval system, or transmitted in any form or by any means, electronic, mechanical, photocopying, recording, or otherwise, without either the prior written permission of the Publishers or a licence permitting restricted copying in the United Kingdom issued by the Copyright Licensing Agency Ltd, 90 Tottenham Court Road, London W1T 4LP (www.cla.co.uk).

Editorial: Emma Lynch, Jilly Attwood and Claire Throp
Design: Jo Hinton-Malivoire and Tokay, Bicester, UK (www.tokay.co.uk)
Picture Research: Rosie Garai and Liz Eddison
Production: Séverine Ribierre

Originated by Ambassador Litho Ltd
Printed in China by WKT Company Ltd

ISBN 0 431 18888 2 (hardback)
08 07 06 05 04
10 9 8 7 6 5 4 3 2 1

ISBN 0 431 18895 5 (paperback)
09 08 07 06 05
10 9 8 7 6 5 4 3 2 1

British Library Cataloguing in Publication Data
Spilsbury, Richard
Bengal tiger - (Animals under threat)
599.7'56
A full catalogue record for this book is available from the British Library.

Acknowledgements
The Publishers would like to thank the following for permission to reproduce photographs: Ardea pp. **4**, **8**, **32** (J. Van Gruisen), **10**, **34** (M. Iljima), **19** (M Watson), **26**, (P Morris), **29**, **38** (McDougal), **31** (Jagdeep Rajput), **33** (John Mason); Bruce Coleman p. **6** (Staffan Widstrand); Corbis pp. **18** (T. Whittaker), **20** (Arvind Garg), **25** (Bagla Pallava), **27** (Adrian Arbib), **30** (Tom Brakefield); Digital Vision pp. **16**, **41**; Ecoscene p. **22** (S Tiwari); FLPA pp. **5** (P Perry), **23** (Silvestris); Getty Images p. **14** (Anup Shah); Nature Picture Library pp. **13**, **17** (Anup Shah), **21** (Ashok Jain; NHPA pp. **9**, **42** (Martin Harvey), **11**, **35** (Andy Rouse); OSF pp. **24** (Malcolm Coe), **28** (Mike Hill), **37** (Austerman); Rex p. **36** (Paul Lovelace); Richard Spilsbury p. **39**; Tudor Photography p. **43**.

Cover photograph reproduced with permission of OSF/Mike Powles.

The publishers would like to thank Dr Chris Tydeman, Environmental Consultant, for his assistance in the preparation of this book.

The author would like to thank Neel Gogate for supplying the map reference for page 15.

Disclaimer
All the Internet addresses (URLs) given in this book were valid at the time of going to press. However, due to the dynamic nature of the Internet, some addresses may have changed, or sites may have ceased to exist since publication. While the author and publishers regret any inconvenience this may cause readers, no responsibility for any such changes can be accepted by either the author or the publishers.

Every effort has been made to contact copyright holders of any material reproduced in this book. Any omissions will be rectified in subsequent printings if notice is given to the publishers.

The paper used to print this book comes from sustainable resources.

Contents

Words printed in the text in bold, **like this**, are explained in the Glossary.

The Bengal tiger

The tiger is the biggest and probably most recognizable cat in the world. Of all the big cats – such as lions, leopards and jaguars – only tigers have stripey coats. Tigers are part of a large group or **genus** called *panthera*, which also includes big cats such as the leopard. All tigers belong to one smaller group or **species** called *tigris*. Within this there are five surviving **subspecies**. Each one gets its name from the different part of Asia where it lives or was first named. The five subspecies are called Bengal, Sumatran, Siberian, South China and Indo-Chinese tigers.

Tigers of each subspecies look slightly different. Siberian tigers are generally biggest – sometimes over 3 metres long – with fewer stripes than other subspecies. Each individual tiger of any subspecies, however, has a unique stripe pattern, a bit like our fingerprints. This means it can be distinguished from any other tiger.

Tiger ancestors

To find the **ancestors** of modern tigers we must look back 60 million years, to the age of the dinosaurs. The small weasel-like **mammals** that lived on Earth at this time were totally different to tigers. Over millions of years, however, their **descendants** gradually became the distinctive bear, dog and cat families we recognize today. Fossil evidence suggests that the earliest tigers appeared two million years ago. Since then, tigers have spread over nearly the whole of Asia.

▲ *Bengal tigers usually have a bright reddish-orange coat, with a creamy white belly. Their thin stripes are mostly vertical and are black, grey or brown.*

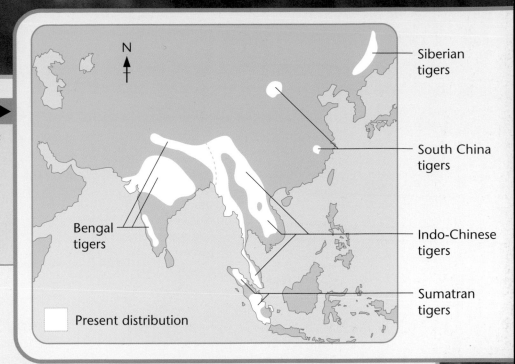

The five subspecies of tiger live in different parts of Asia. The Bengal tiger is the commonest.

Siberian tigers

South China tigers

Indo-Chinese tigers

Sumatran tigers

Bengal tigers

Present distribution

Changing fortunes

Tens of thousands of years ago, the tiger species was one of the most dominant of the major **predators** of Asia. Like all animals, they lived more successfully in some areas than others, for reasons such as changes in climate and availability of **prey**. Over time, tigers became sufficiently different from each other in different areas for eight separate subspecies to be distinguished.

Populations of all eight tiger subspecies remained stable for a long time – that is until humans started to kill them in large numbers, by hunting and by changing the places where they lived. In the last hundred years, three of the subspecies – the Caspian, Bali and Java tigers – have become **extinct** because of our activities. All the remaining subspecies of tiger are **endangered**. This means that unless we take special care to look after them, they could also become extinct. The rarest, the South China tiger, has a wild population of only around 20–30 tigers and is on the edge of disappearing for ever.

Bengal tigers

This book focuses on Bengal tigers, first named in the state of Bengal in western India. There are more wild Bengal tigers than tigers of all the other subspecies put together, but their population is falling each year. Many people are already trying to protect them. By examining the lives and habits of these big cats, and the threats they face, the book also shows what we can do to save the tigers on our planet.

Nearly all wild Bengal tigers live in India. The Bengal tiger is often called the Indian tiger. Some Bengal tigers live outside India in neighbouring countries. There are small populations in southern Nepal, western Burma, Bhutan and Bangladesh.

Tiger habitat

Bengal tigers live in a range of different **habitats** in these countries, but all the habitats have certain features in common. A suitable tiger habitat must provide some type of dense plant cover. Something to hide behind is vital for this **predator**, so it can **stalk** its **prey** without being seen. Tiger habitat must also provide the large amounts of food and water they need to survive.

Tigers in India

There are populations of Bengal tigers in 18 of the 26 states, or regions, of India.

About a third of all Bengal tigers live in the central Indian state of Madhya Pradesh.

Madhya Pradesh contains around one-fifth of India's forest area and large populations of gaur, a favourite tiger prey.

For a tiger to survive, it must live in the same habitats as the animals that it feeds upon.

Bengal tigers can live in different kinds of forest. Some live in humid, **tropical** forests with thick, lush undergrowth, often called jungle. Others live among tall grasses such as bamboo, or in open **deciduous** woodland. These types of habitat change more noticeably with the seasons, especially in the annual rainy season called the **monsoon**.

Bengal tigers have adapted to life in different types of climate. Some live in Himalayan valleys 3000 metres above sea level that are annually cloaked in thick snow. Others live in hot, mosquito-infested swamps, or in dry **scrub** areas on the edge of deserts.

Sundarbans tigers

The Sundarbans is a swampy area where the land meets the sea, near the mouth of the Ganges River in eastern India. The habitat is one of wooded islands and areas of mangrove swamps. Mangroves are plants that thrive in seawater. Their tangled roots stick out of the thick, salty mud. Many young fish and crabs live in the warm shallow water among the mangroves. These are prey for many birds and crocodiles. Several hundred tigers also live in this unusual habitat. They are strong swimmers, so they can travel between the many small islands in search of prey and shelter.

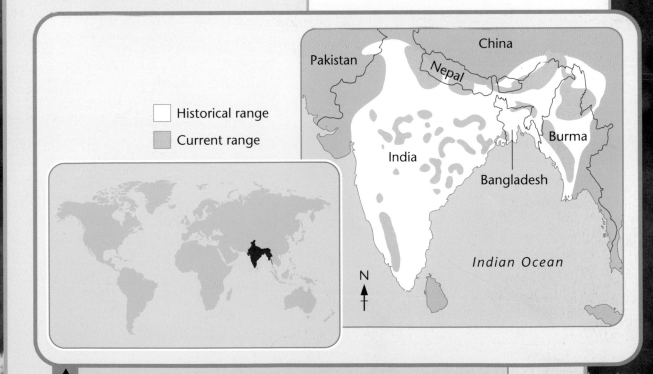

Historical range

Current range

China
Pakistan
Nepal
Burma
India
Bangladesh
Indian Ocean
N

Bengal tigers now live only in patches of population throughout India and neighbouring countries.

There is much debate about how many Bengal tigers there are in the wild. Most scientists estimate that there are between 3200 and 4500. Over 2500 of these are in India. With so few tigers, you might think that they could be counted quite accurately. The problem is that although they are big **mammals**, tigers are fairly secretive. They move around mostly at night, often in dense woodland, and they are good at hiding. So how do scientists estimate how many tigers there are?

The stripes on a tiger help to keep its large body hidden in the vertical shade patches between tall plants.

Signs of tigers

The best way to find out if tigers are around is to look for signs they have left. These might be leftover parts of **carcasses** from their kills, piles of dung, or pugmarks (footprints). But the presence of these signs does not help us to know how many tigers made them. One thing we do know is that there is a limit to how many kills one tiger makes in a short period of time. So, a lot of carcasses spread over a wide area may mean that many tigers are around.

Scientists make more accurate estimates of numbers of tigers by using pugmarks to recognize individuals. Tigers have big fleshy pads on their paws, which cushion their feet and help them to walk quietly when hunting. The pads on an individual's feet are different in shape, size and number of scratches or cuts to those of others. This makes each tiger's pugmarks slightly different.

Identifying pugmarks

Scientists who study tiger populations record information about the pugmarks they find in an area. People skilled in **tracking** wild animals often help them. The scientists usually take photos or make sketches of the pugmarks. Sometimes they take plaster casts of them.

It takes a lot of experience and training to spot small differences between pugmarks. To help identification, scientists build up computer databases of pugmark images belonging to particular tigers. They can take these databases on portable computers out into the study area when tracking.

The problem with pugmarks is that they can only be seen clearly on certain types of ground. They are visible in damp mud, but not in dry grass or fallen leaves. So they cannot be used to recognize tigers in certain **habitats**. It is also expensive to hire enough trackers to look for pugmarks in every part of a study area.

▲ *The plaster cast of an old pugmark is compared with new pugmarks to check which tiger has passed through.*

Controversy

There has long been controversy over the method of monitoring tiger populations by counting pugmarks, but recently a small group of scientists have claimed the process should not be continued. They say it is misleading because only a small area of tiger habitat is searched properly, while in some conditions pugmarks are impossible to locate. Their findings have encouraged the Indian government to look at new methods. However, in the short term at least, the pugmark approach will continue to be used.

Bengal tigers have a range of special features that help them survive in their **habitat**. Adults can be nearly 3 metres long and weigh over 200 kilograms but, like most cats, they are very muscular and agile, with good balance. They can leap up to 10 metres, swim several kilometres and occasionally climb trees. A tiger's legs are thick and strong, with paws up to 30 centimetres across. Each paw has four large toes, and the front paws have a fifth smaller one higher up the leg. A sharp, curved claw sticks out of each toe when the tiger stretches its paws. Claws are used to hold on to the tiger's **prey** and to scratch. The claws tuck back in when not in use, to stop them being worn or damaged.

A tiger's mouth

Tigers are **carnivores**, with short and powerful jaws. They have 30 large teeth. The four long, pointed canine teeth are used for stabbing and gripping prey, and are up to 9 centimetres long. Wider carnassial teeth at the back of the jaw have sharp ridges that help cut through flesh and bone. A tiger's tongue is long and coated with tiny, sharp bumps. These bumps make it rough enough, when used with force, to lick hair or even skin off prey. A tiger also uses its tongue more gently to groom (comb and lick) its own hair, and to lap up water to drink.

Tigers pull back their cheeks and lips to expose their formidable canine teeth.

Tiger senses

Tigers use their senses to understand and react to the world around them, just like us. Two of their senses – sight and hearing – are especially well developed.

Tigers' eyes point forwards, like those of many **predators**. This allows them to see what is moving in front of them and judge how far away it is. This is called binocular vision. Many prey animals have eyes on the sides of their heads, so they can see all around them to spot predators approaching. Tigers' vision at night, when they usually hunt, is about six times better than ours. This is because they have a reflective coating inside their eyes that reflects the small amount of light onto their sensitive **retinas**.

Tigers, like other cats, have acute hearing that can pick up very soft sounds. They can tell whether leaves in the undergrowth are rustling because of a breeze or because an animal is brushing against them. They can twist their ears in the direction of sounds, to locate possible prey quickly.

A cat's whiskers

Whiskers are thick, sensitive hairs that grow most obviously on a cat's upper lip, but also above its eyes and on other parts of its body. Cats use their whiskers mostly at night, to help feel where objects are, including prey, and to judge the width of spaces they are moving through.

If whiskers above its eyes are touched by struggling prey, a tiger closes its eyes for protection. Whiskers around its mouth give advance warning of where to bite.

Types of prey

Bengal tigers usually hunt wild deer – called chital or sambar – and wild pigs, which are often much smaller than themselves. They can also hunt much larger **mammals**, such as water buffalo and a type of Indian wild cattle called a gaur, which is up to 2 metres tall. Tigers are not particularly fussy eaters. They occasionally catch crocodiles, bears, leopards, porcupines, fish, birds or even locusts.

Adult Bengal tigers are not hunted by any other animals. They are called apex **predators**. That means they are at the top of the **food web** in their **habitat**. Tigers hunt a wide range of **prey** in order to get enough to eat. They hunt mostly at night, in the early morning or late evening.

Tigers take easy options if they can, usually hunting slower-moving, weaker prey. They prefer larger prey if it is available.

How tigers hunt

Tigers hunt on their own. They look out for prey from the cover of bushes, trees and long grass. When they spot a suitable victim, they carefully **stalk** closer. When stalking, a tiger keeps its head steady, with its eyes focused on its prey, and its body low. It stays down-wind, because a whiff of tiger scent would alert the prey to its presence.

Bengal tigers are at the top of the food web.

The powerful throat grip of a Bengal tiger crushes the throat of this chital deer.

The rush

When the tiger is close enough to its prey it suddenly rushes at it, using its long, heavy tail to keep its balance as the prey changes direction. If the tiger attacks from too far away, the prey will probably escape, because tigers can run fast only over short distances of up to about 25 metres.

Tigers are excellent hunters, but only one out of ten tiger rushes is successful. When the rush is timed properly, the tiger uses its strong front legs and sharp claws to grab the back of the neck, shoulders or chest of its prey. If the prey is big, the tiger may grab its ankles to trip it up. Once the prey has been brought down, the tiger switches to a throat grip, which **suffocates** the prey. Smaller prey are killed with a bite to the back of their neck.

The carcass

Tigers carry or drag the prey's **carcass** to shelter or near water, over distances of up to 500 metres. Tigers eat all parts of the carcass. They eat up to 40 kilograms of meat at one meal, but usually makes a kill only every three or four days. After eating they often have a drink of water. If any of the carcass is left over, they hide it under grass or leaves and come back to it later.

Nearly all cats are solitary animals – they spend most of their time alone. Each adult tiger lives in a particular area of its **habitat** all year round. This area provides it with enough food, shelter and water holes. It is called a **home range**.

Bengal tigers, like other big cats, live in large home ranges of between 10 and 250 square kilometres. A home range is usually smaller in areas where there is plenty of **prey**, but larger where prey animals are fewer. Home ranges can also change in size during the year. For example, Bengal tigers that live by the Himalayas move through a bigger area during the snowy winter than they do in summer, to find enough prey.

Keeping other tigers out

A tiger will generally try to keep other tigers out of its home range, or part of it. An area that an animal keeps other animals out of is called a **territory**. A tiger makes a territory so it has exclusive rights, not only to the prey in it but also to any **breeding** opportunities. Males make territories because they contain females they want to mate with. There may be several female home ranges within one male's territory. Females have territories to keep other tigers away from their cubs, because they may harm them.

A water hole is an important part of a Bengal tiger's home range. It uses the water to drink and to cool down in. The water may also attract prey.

Working out ranges

Scientists work out tiger ranges by drugging individual tigers so they go to sleep, and fitting them with radio collars. After the animal wakes up, its movements can be followed using radio receivers, and its location marked on a map. Over time, a pattern of regular movement becomes clear and range boundaries can be identified.

In Panna Tiger Reserve, three females live within the home range of one male.

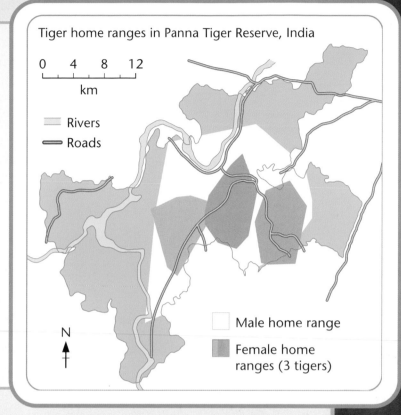

Tiger home ranges in Panna Tiger Reserve, India

0   4   8   12
km

Rivers
Roads

N

Male home range

Female home ranges (3 tigers)

Marking territories

Tigers, like most other cats, **mark** their territories to show others where the boundaries are. They mostly mark with scent. They spray urine on tree trunks or rocks and leave piles of dung, called scats. Sometimes they mark using visual signs. They scratch tree trunks with their claws, or scrape together piles of loose leaves and soil. To make sure other tigers do not miss these signs, they often use visual and scent signals together. When tigers scratch a tree, they also rub it with a scent made in **glands** between their toes.

Once boundaries are marked, tigers patrol them by walking along the scent trails. They may top up any smells that are fading.

No range

Tigers establish their home ranges on a first-come-first-served basis. Some tigers, especially young adult males, will not have a home range until an existing range owner dies. They live in small zones between ranges, keeping out of the way of other tigers. However, young adult females sometimes share a home range with their mother.

Courtship and communication

Roaring

Like other big cats, a tiger uses muscles and elastic ligaments to stretch its throat wide open to make loud roars. It twists its ears back and narrows its eyes as it roars.

A tiger's roar can be heard up to 3 kilometres away.

The **breeding** season for tigers, as for many other animals, is a time of tension. Young adult males will only breed if they have their own **territory**, so they are more likely to risk entering another male's territory at this time.

The breeding cycle begins with courtship, when animals select and attract a mate. Tigresses (female tigers) first go into oestrus. This means they are on heat and ready to mate. They communicate their condition by roaring and moaning repeatedly. They also **mark** their territory with a mixture of urine and fluid from special **glands**.

The male tiger whose territory the female is in regularly smells scent marks left by other tigers. However, the scent left by a female in oestrus is different, and he responds in a special way. His face goes into a grimace: his nose wrinkles, his eyes close, his chin is raised, his mouth opens and his tongue lolls out. He is testing the scent using a sensitive pit in the roof of his mouth called the Jacobson's organ.

Tigers communicate their feelings and intentions in different ways including body language. The position of their ears shows how tense they are. The white spots on the back of their ears help other tigers identify their ear position.

16

Rival males

The oestrus signals made by a female may attract more than one male. If two males meet, one – normally the trespasser – backs away. Sometimes both stay put and test each other's nerve with a series of displays – each with a particular meaning. They challenge each other first by staring, then by showing their teeth and flaring their whiskers. If neither backs down, they move on to hissing and increasingly loud growling. Tigers usually rely on display to sort out arguments, because fighting with their sharp claws, teeth and immense strength could easily result in serious injury or death.

Meeting a mate

When a male and a female meet up to mate, they are very wary at first. These solitary animals are not often in the company of strangers. They snarl and snap at each other for a while, moving gradually closer. Eventually the female trusts the male enough to start to nuzzle, lick and rub him. She is now ready to mate.

Seasonal breeding

Bengal tigers enjoy a season of plenty during the Indian autumn. The spring to summer **monsoon** rains have watered the dry land, encouraging many plants to grow. Like most animals, **herbivores**, such as deer, use the period of plentiful food to breed. As a result, prey is plentiful for tigers in autumn and winter, and they too can breed. They usually mate between November and April. They give birth three to four months later.

Bengal tigers rear up on their back legs to fight using their claws and teeth.

Young tigers

Pregnant tigresses usually give birth to two or three cubs. A mother chooses a lair – a safe, sheltered spot to give birth. It may be in a cave, a rocky crevice or space within dense plant cover. The newborn cubs are covered in short stripey hair and weigh around 1 kilogram each. Their eyes are closed, and do not open until they are around two weeks old. The first danger they face is starvation. Although their mother cares for them by licking their coats clean, she does not help them **suckle**. It can take a cub up to four hours to find a nipple.

A tigress's milk is a complete food for her cubs for the first eight weeks of life. It helps the cubs grow and develop quickly and even provides the water they need.

Growing up

Cubs start to come out of the lair when their eyes open. They are inquisitive but also cautious, and stay close to their mother. If she leaves them to hunt, she makes sure they are somewhere safe, such as the old lair or a new shelter. As they cannot walk very fast, she often carries the cubs by gripping the loose skin on their necks and head in her teeth.

The cubs start to eat meat brought by their mother when they are around two months old. They suckle less and less, until they stop altogether around four months later.

Independence

The cubs learn to hunt food for themselves in stages. At first their mother brings a **carcass** to them to eat. She may help by ripping open tough skin to reveal the softer meat inside. Later, she partly kills an animal and they learn how to kill with a **suffocating** hold. Finally, the cubs start to hunt small **prey**, improving their technique mostly by watching their mother but sometimes also their father. Cubs become independent of their mother at between eighteen months and two years, when they usually find their own **home ranges**.

Natural dangers

Tiger cubs face many natural dangers, from **predators** to fires and floods. About half of all cubs do not survive more than two years. A cub away from the safety of its mother, or out of hiding, may become prey for a hyena, a leopard or a wild dog. Cubs are sometimes killed by adult male tigers trying to take over **territory** belonging to the cubs' father. As the cubs grow, some of these dangers lessen. Tigers may live for as long as 20 years.

Runt of the litter

One cub, called the runt, is usually smaller than the others. Some runts die at birth, but many others die later through starvation or being easier prey for predators.

Play is a vital way for tiger cubs to learn how to survive as adults. Rough and tumble like this helps them develop useful hunting skills.

Conflict between tigers and people

Adult Bengal tigers face no wild **predators** unless they are weakened by injury, illness or old age. However, there is one **species** that is so dangerous that all tigers, whatever their age and strength, are at risk: human beings.

A human might not appear to be much of a threat to a tiger. An adult tiger is bigger, stronger and equipped with far more lethal natural weapons – teeth and claws. However, people have developed weapons that can kill any tiger, and machines that can completely change a tiger's **habitat**. These dangers from people are not faced by Bengal tigers alone – many other wild animals are also at risk. There is usually one major reason why animals become **endangered** – people want to take over or use the wild places where they live.

Population explosion

There are more than six billion people on Earth. The population is expanding rapidly, and is predicted to reach seven billion by 2015. There are many reasons for this. One is improvements in healthcare, which mean more diseases can be cured and illnesses treated, so more babies survive and older people live longer. As the population increases, people need more space to live, work and get food and water. This means they put more pressure on the environment.

When people cut down forest to plant crops or graze animals, there is less space for tigers and their prey.

Fishermen in the Sundarbans often wear human face masks in the hope of frightening off a maneating tiger approaching from behind.

Conflict

As areas of the Bengal tiger's habitat get smaller, the tigers find it more and more difficult to find enough food. As people and tigers live closer together, conflicts and problems arise. **Livestock**, such as cattle, buffalo or goats, which people keep on newly cleared land or in enclosed areas, are easy **prey** for hungry tigers. A tiger's stealth and hunting skills mean it can get past most human guards. Some tigers even become accustomed to eating mostly livestock, because it takes less effort to catch than trying to **stalk** and rush wild pigs and other quick prey. People try to scare off tigers by moving in large groups through the forest carrying lit torches or banging drums. If this does not scare off the tigers, people sometimes kill them.

Maneaters

Some tigers get so desperate for a meal that they prey on people. Maneaters are usually tigers that are too old or injured to hunt, but they can also be fitter, younger animals. Catching unarmed people is easier than hunting stronger, faster wild animals. Maneating tigers are rare, but they often kill more than once. There are several known maneaters in the Sundarbans National Park in India that have often killed fishermen and collectors of wild honey.

Poaching

Poaching means illegally killing or taking wild animals. One example is fishing salmon from a stretch of river that belongs to someone else. Another is killing **endangered** Bengal tigers in protected **reserves**.

It is difficult to know how many tigers are poached, because no-one knows exactly what the population is, and poachers are secretive. Nevertheless, it is estimated that one Bengal tiger is killed every day.

Why people poach

People poach Bengal tigers because illegal traders have offered them money for tigers' skin, bones and other body parts. The traders approach people who are poor and who live in or near areas where tigers live, because they have detailed knowledge of the **habitat**. The poachers need the money, so they are prepared to risk the punishment of being fined and jailed.

How people poach

Poachers use various ways to kill tigers. The commonest way is to put poison in fresh **carcasses** of **livestock** such as cows or buffalo. In dry seasons they poison the water in small forest pools where tigers drink.

Poaching is one of the main reasons why Bengal tigers are endangered.

The risk and the reward

- A poacher is paid around £30 for killing a tiger. A trader can sell the tiger parts for £2000–£4000.
- If someone is caught poaching a tiger, the penalty for breaking the law is a fine of around £100 and a minimum of one year in jail. Because of difficulties enforcing laws, only one or two people have ever been convicted of killing a tiger in India.

Special steel traps are also used. They are set along trails where tigers might walk and covered over so they cannot be seen. If a tiger steps in a trap it closes on its leg, usually injuring the tiger so badly that it dies.

One in ten

One adult tiger contains around 17 kilograms of bone. This makes a year's supply of traditional rheumatism medicine tablets for just ten people.

In some areas, poachers use hidden electrical wires to electrocute tigers. They also use guns in remote parts of reserves where the gunshots cannot be heard by **wardens**.

Smuggling routes

The valuable parts of the tiger are **smuggled** to where they can be sold. Tiger bones are often hidden among those from legally killed animals, such as cattle. The bones are used to make glue and fertilizers (nutrients used to make plants grow better).

Traders smuggle Bengal tiger parts from India into China across the mountains. They trade them with Tibetan nomads (travelling people), who in turn sell them to traditional medicine makers in China.

Tiger parts are highly valued in traditional medicines. Bones are ground into powder and made into pills and potions to treat rheumatism and weakness. Eyeballs are used to treat epilepsy, and whiskers for toothache. Tiger medicines are sold illegally in shops and clinics around the world.

▲ *Tiger traps can be so strong that they take six adult men to open them.*

Dealing with poaching

In many places in India, tigers are protected in **reserves**. **Wardens** and guards patrol the reserves to keep **poachers** away. However, the poachers are often better equipped than the guards, and can be very dangerous. They have guns and explosives, and fast vehicles to get away quickly. They commonly use mobile phones to warn each other of possible detection.

There are also often only a few wardens for each reserve, making it difficult to find the poachers. This problem is sometimes made worse when local people help poachers. They may help **track** tigers, or protect the poachers. This may be because they are frightened of them, or have been paid to help, or because their **livestock** will be safer with fewer tigers about.

Stopping poachers

Poaching can be stopped, but it takes money to equip and employ reserve workers. Reserve workers should be encouraged to arrest poachers and seize dead tiger parts, to stop them being sold. Any dead tigers found should be examined carefully to see if they were poisoned or died naturally. The best long-term solution is to encourage both poachers and local people to change their attitudes and look after the tigers.

Reserves are only effective protection for tigers if there are enough wardens and they have good equipment.

Stopping the bone traders

The trade in Bengal tiger bones had become a major problem in India by the 1980s. Populations of other **subspecies** of tiger, in countries such as China, were falling. Demand was growing for traditional medicines made with tiger parts, so poaching increased elsewhere. Some traders in tiger parts are rich businessmen who have connections with important people in different countries. This often allows them to avoid capture and punishment.

The bones, skins and claws of around 250 tigers have been seized in India since 1993.

The best way to stop international traders is to use the law. Undercover investigators make contact with traders and track their **smuggling** routes. They inform police and **customs** officers, who seize and destroy tiger parts and punish the traders. However, international laws have to be agreed and enforced worldwide, to punish international traders more strictly so they stop trading. It would help investigators if they could use the latest ways of distinguishing between tiger and cattle bones, such as DNA (**gene**) testing.

changing demand

Tiger medicines are in demand partly because they are an alternative to Western medicines, but also because they are a traditional custom. People all over the world, including doctors and scientists, say that tiger parts are no more effective as cures than, say, buffalo parts. They say that it is time to change a tradition that is threatening tigers with **extinction**.

Tiger hunting in the past

In the past people hunted tigers for different reasons. Some people were paid to kill tigers so as to protect other people. In India in the 18th and 19th centuries there were professional tiger hunters called shikaris. They made their living by accompanying travellers through tiger **habitats**, and by helping villagers get rid of tigers. They often wore a tiger skin, which they claimed gave them magical powers, and carried a shield, a spear or a sword. Shikaris built platforms in trees called machans, where they would wait to spear tigers. They also dug and covered over pit traps containing spears, for unsuspecting tigers to fall into.

Sport of kings

Tiger hunting was also a royal sport. To Indian kings, killing a tiger was a proof of their power. Ancient custom decreed that a ruler should kill 109 tigers to make the grade! Kings never hunted alone – hundreds or even thousands of helpers made sure the hunt would be successful. The king often rode on the back of an elephant, in an ornate saddle platform called a howdah. Some helpers rode on other elephants, loading rifles for the king. Others, called beaters, walked in groups through the forest or grass shouting, letting off fireworks or beating drums. Their noise flushed out any wild animals, including tigers, from the dense vegetation towards the king and others with guns.

During the 19th century Europeans, including the British, began tiger hunting in the style of the Indian kings.

British in India

To the British people who came to India as **colonizers** in the early 19th century, hunting tigers was partly seen as a public service. They had more reliable and powerful guns than the locals, so they were more likely to be successful. Locals looked to British soldiers or policemen to act as shikaris. Some skilled shikaris became legendary, because they removed well-known maneaters.

In the later 19th century and early 20th century, tiger hunting became a popular sport among rich British people in India. Hunts were also big social events, like parties, and people competed over who could shoot the most tigers. It was not unusual for people to kill over 100 tigers each. To show their bravery they proudly displayed their catches, such as tiger skins with stuffed heads displaying snarling teeth, which they used as rugs. As the craze for these items, and for fashions using tiger skin, spread to Europe and other parts of the world, the tiger population fell rapidly.

Tiger hunting is not just a thing of the past. Even today, some people think tiger skin rugs are impressive trophies.

Shooting film not bullets

Jim Corbett grew up in India, learnt to shoot well and killed his first tiger at the age of eight. He later became famous as a shikari. He **tracked** and killed the 'Champawat Tiger', a maneater that had killed over 400 people. Corbett killed many tigers, but he also learnt about them, and increasingly took photos rather than shots. In 1936, distressed at how rare they were becoming, he set up the Corbett National Park in India to help conserve tigers.

Destroying tiger habitats

One of the greatest threats to Bengal tigers, after **poaching**, is the destruction of their **habitat**. In the past, Asia was covered in large areas of forest. Today most of this forest has disappeared as a direct result of the growing human population. Between 1973 and 2003, the number of people in India rose by nearly 500 million and the number of **livestock** by 100 million.

Many trees and other plants are cut down for building timber, for firewood fuel and for livestock food. Other areas are cleared to provide land for farming and housing. Farms and houses need water and power, so yet more land is cleared to build dams and canals for **irrigation**, power plants for electricity, and roads to move around on. Habitat is also destroyed to dig mines and build factories. Some of these industries add to the problems for wild animals, by **polluting** rivers, lakes and the air.

For some people, forests are simply a supply of wood they can fell and sell, not special habitats occupied by different plants and animals.

The price of development

Many people see habitat destruction as an acceptable result of **development**, which improves the lives of others. For example, building a factory on newly cleared land may bring jobs to the local people. Thus, a lot of habitat destruction is officially approved. In 2000, the Indian government approved a project with funding from the World Bank to build the Kotku Dam, which will provide water, power and jobs for local people. However, it will also drown the best forests in a tiger reserve called Palamau.

Bengal tigers are running out of habitat in India.

The importance of tiger habitat

Tiger habitats are important to the environment for several reasons. One of the most critical reasons is water. Forests and jungle in India are prime **water catchment areas**. When rain falls onto forests and their surrounding hills, it soaks into the topsoil – the ground's fertile surface. Some water filters into rivers, water holes and dams, but some filters into the ground. This groundwater provides water for wells used by many Indian people. Without trees, topsoil washes away and rainwater runs off the hills, often causing flooding and not topping up groundwater supplies.

Tiger habitat is also vital for many other animals and plants that in turn benefit humans. For example, local people harvest seasonal foods such as honey and fruit, and plants that can be used as medicines.

Links in a food chain

A Bengal tiger's survival is linked with the lives of other organisms in its habitat. Tigers will only have enough **prey** to hunt if the prey can find enough to eat. Deer, for example, need grass, tender shoots and wild fruit to eat. Tigers and other **predators** are useful to prey groups. When they hunt weaker, diseased or older members of a herd of prey, the fitter, stronger survivors breed and improve the overall health of the herd.

Fragmented tiger populations

Today, the remaining wild Bengal tigers live in many different places. All patches of tiger **habitat** are surrounded by land that they cannot live on. This may be because the land has been **developed**, for example with roads and towns, or because people have hunted most of the wild pigs and deer, so there is not enough **prey** for tigers.

Fragments

In the past, areas where tigers lived covered vast areas. Along the border between India and Nepal, for example, there used to be thousands of kilometres of continuous forest where tigers lived. Today, there are four separate populations, each with between 45 and 15 tigers, cut off from each other by farms and villages. The tigers in these fragmented populations cannot mix. It is as if they are trapped on islands surrounded by expanses of ocean, and are unable to swim.

▲ *Small, isolated populations of Bengal tigers are at risk of becoming lost for ever. Many kinds of chance event, such as a drought or a flood, could wipe them out.*

▲ When animals like tigers are split up into small groups they face even more danger of extinction. People can help by creating corridors – narrow strips – of suitable habitat between the populations of tigers. Tigers can then travel from one area to another to breed.

Too small

There can be problems within small populations of tigers. If there are only a few males, if one dies there may not be enough other males around to mate with the females, so they will not have cubs. If there are more males in the population, they are more likely to fight and be injured as they attempt to control more of the available space.

When tigers in an isolated population breed just with each other (**inbreed**) over several generations, the tiger population becomes weaker, or less able to survive changes. This is because they begin to have very similar **genes**. For example, if a disease spreads through the group and all the tigers share a low resistance to it, they might all die. If there is more variety in the genes within the group, some tigers will be affected less than others. These tigers will survive, and pass on their resistance to their young.

Inbred tigers become weaker in different ways. Some are infertile (unable to breed) and others have physical problems, such as crossed eyes or cleft palates (a split in the roof of the mouth), that affect their ability to hunt.

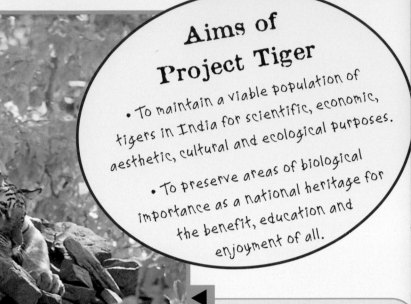

Aims of Project Tiger

• To maintain a viable population of tigers in India for scientific, economic, aesthetic, cultural and ecological purposes.

• To preserve areas of biological importance as a national heritage for the benefit, education and enjoyment of all.

Bengal tigers are protected amongst the ruined palace walls in Ranthambhore Tiger Reserve, India.

In India, there is a long tradition of preserving areas of Bengal tiger **habitat**. In the past this was to keep the areas well stocked with wild animals, like tigers, exclusively for kings and other important people to hunt. In modern times, these areas are preserved to keep out the **poachers** and land **developers**, to save the wild animals.

Project Tiger

A tiger population survey in 1972 confirmed the worst fears of international conservation workers – there were fewer than 2000 Bengal tigers left in India. In 1973 Project Tiger was launched by the Indian government, with the support of international conservation organizations such as WWF and IUCN (The World Conservation Union). The tiger became India's new national symbol. Nine tiger **reserves** were set up, and more followed in later years. Each reserve is patrolled by **wardens** to stop poaching. The initial hope was that tiger populations in these areas would increase, and that eventually tigers would spread out into the surrounding areas.

Changing emphasis

When Project Tiger reserves were set up, local people living in these areas were badly affected. Often they had to move their homes to new places. They were not allowed to work in or collect wild food from the forests, as they traditionally had, because the land was given over to tigers. This created frustration and resentment about the reserves. Over time, it has become clear that people have increasingly moved back into these reserves, squeezing the tigers out.

In recent years the emphasis of Project Tiger has changed. More effort is now made to develop the habitat around tiger reserves for local people, in a non-destructive way. This is called ecodevelopment. For example, Project Tiger and other conservation groups work with local people to set up dams and irrigation systems, so they can get the water they need without taking it from reserves. They help to install solar-powered lighting around the villages, to keep tigers away from people's **livestock**.

Project Tiger

There are now 23 Project Tiger reserves, and they make up about one third of the protected areas where tigers live in India. Between 1976 and 1979, twelve villages were resettled when Ranthambhore National Park was set up.

People plant fast-growing plants for fuel and animal feed, so they do not have to cut down slow-growing plants in the tiger reserves. These workers are irrigating the fields.

Conservation organizations

Project Tiger **reserves**, and the national parks in places where Bengal tigers live, need money and expert assistance to keep going. They rely on help from national and local government, and also from international aid. For example, in 1994 the US Congress passed a Tiger Conservation Act, offering funds to support **development** in other countries that are sympathetic to tiger conservation.

Tiger conservation also relies on a wide range of non-governmental organizations (NGOs), including charities. Whether local, national or international, most of these organizations raise money for conservation from donations by the public or businesses. For example, an NGO called the National Fish and Wildlife Foundation persuaded the oil company Exxon to pledge over £600,000 to the US 'Save the Tiger Fund'. NGOs and charities sometimes work together with governments, for example if they can offer scientific expertise about tigers. Charities do not make any financial profit from their work, and rely on help from many unpaid volunteers as well as their paid workers. As they are financially independent, they sometimes protest against government action, such as the destruction of **habitat** caused by development.

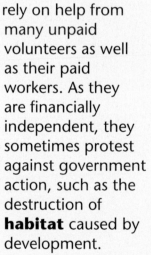

Scientific experts from NGOs and charities study tigers, to help in their conservation. This tiger has been tranquillized so a radiocollar can be fitted.

These traditional medicines advertise that they contain tiger. The efforts of conservation organizations have helped to ban their sale.

Conserving Bengal tigers

Tigers are impressive animals, and their problems have led to the creation of many conservation groups and major **campaigns** (some of these are mentioned on page 46). Some are local in their aims, such as conserving tigers in a particular area, but others are more wide-ranging. In 1975 the Convention on International Trade in Endangered Species (CITES, pronounced 'sightease') was formed to control and regulate the trade in **endangered** animals. Campaigns at this time focused on trying to stop people wearing big-cat fur as fashion, such as fur coats.

How endangered?

Conservation specialists at CITES divide endangered animals into three different categories, depending on how much protection they need. Tigers are ranked CITES Appendix 1, which means they are at risk of extinction within five years and any trade in tigers is illegal.

More recently, WWF and TRAFFIC worked with the US Congress to establish the 1998 US Rhino and Tiger Product Labeling Act. Just under half of the shops surveyed in Chinatowns in seven cities in the US and Canada sold medicines labelled as containing tiger parts. Previous laws had only made the distribution of these medicines illegal. The new act made it illegal to sell *any* product containing or claiming to contain tiger parts. In this way, consumers can legally buy only traditional medicines made by responsible manufacturers who do not use illegal ingredients.

People have caged and enclosed big cats for thousands of years. In the past, zoos simply provided the spectacle of seeing exotic and dangerous animals in cramped cages. The zoos and wildlife parks of today are very different.

Information and conservation

Modern zoos and wildlife parks enable visitors to study tigers close-up, in cages and enclosures that are as much as possible like their **habitat**. Visitors can learn more about tigers from information displays, multimedia presentations and libraries. Money raised from entrance tickets, gift shops and by fundraising, is used not only to look after the captive animals, but also to help with the conservation of tigers in the wild. Zoos work closely with conservation groups, **reserve** workers and governments to help look after wild Bengal tigers and their habitats.

Zoo facts

There are about 1200 tigers in zoos around the world.

Adult tigers in zoos eat horse meat supplemented with egg, yeast and vitamins.

Tigers are expensive to keep in captivity. It costs up to £2000 a year for each tiger.

Breeding programmes

Many zoos have **breeding** programmes for **endangered** animals like tigers. A male from one zoo will be lent to another zoo, to mate with a female. Breeding programmes are important for providing zoos with enough tigers, so that no more are taken from the wild. They also bring money into the zoo, from visitors wanting to see baby tigers. This can lead to a surplus of tigers in captivity, as zoos breed animals to get this visitor money.

◀

Captive tigers need keepers to feed them. This cub is being bottle-fed, because his mother could not make enough milk.

White tigers are unusual Bengal tigers with creamy white fur, chocolate stripes and blue eyes.

Tiger breeding programmes need to be carefully monitored to avoid **inbreeding**. When any captive tiger breeds with another it is recorded in an internationally-available 'tiger studbook'. Any zoo can then check up on a tiger's background. There are only just over 330 Bengal tigers in captivity, mostly in Indian zoos. Some other tigers claimed to be Bengals are actually a mixture of Bengal and another tiger **subspecies**.

Reintroduction

Breeding programmes are also important for reintroducing some endangered species back into the wild. This is successful for some animals, but not for others. Tigers, like other big cats, cannot be reintroduced. This is mainly because they are **predators**. They survive by hunting, and if they have been reared in captivity, where they are fed and confined, they will not have learned how to hunt. A reintroduced tiger would also not be resistant to diseases, or aware of **territory** and the associated dangers of other tigers.

white tigers

White tigers are Bengal tigers that are not orange and black! There are around 40 in captivity. Most are inbred **descendants** of a wild white tiger called Mohan, caught in 1951. If a white tiger was born in the wild, it would probably not survive long because its colour would not conceal it effectively when **stalking prey**.

Tiger tourism and local people

To see a tiger in the wild would be high on the wish-list of many animal lovers. Tiger tourism is an important business in India. Private tour companies, national parks and **reserves** earn valuable income from tourism. Some of this money helps conserve tigers and other wildlife, but many conservationists say tourism is the latest severe danger for Bengal tigers.

Tourism can help in the conservation of tigers, but it must be carried out responsibly.

Tourist pressure

Irresponsible tourism can create big problems for tigers, their **habitats** and the people who live near by. Visitors demand facilities such as hotels, lodges and restaurants. These use up local resources like building materials, water, food and power, affecting life for local people. The price of these resources and of land sometimes rises so much that local people cannot afford to live there.

Big hotel groups can easily afford to buy land. They often bring their own staff, so offer no jobs to local people. They contribute little to the local economy, importing expensive fittings for the hotels, food for their restaurants and even forest guides from elsewhere.

Tourism also generates large amounts of waste, such as litter and sewage, that can **pollute** tiger habitat. Increased traffic on roads from private cars and tour buses pollutes the air and increases roadkills. Increased noise from visitors may scare off the wildlife.

Tourists in Periyar benefit from the experience of local guides.

Solutions

Bad tourism excludes local people and leaves them with problems to clear up. This can make them less caring of tiger habitat and wildlife. These days, a different sort of tourism, called **ecotourism**, is promoted by conservation groups. This is small-scale tourism that involves local people and has a low impact on the environment. If local people get rewards from tourism, they will become the guardians rather than the enemies of nature. Governments sometimes encourage ecotourism by reducing taxes for small-scale tourism and increasing taxes for big hotel groups.

Making tourism work in Periyar

The Periyar National Park in the state of Kerala, India, is home to a pioneering ecotourism project. Local people involved in the Periyar Tiger Trail project used to live in the forest, where they made a living by illegally cutting and selling wild cinnamon bark. They are now partners in the protection of Periyar. They use their detailed knowledge of the area to guide small-group treks around the reserve. As they know the area, they are more likely to give visitors the chance to see tigers and other wildlife. The Tiger Trail workers make such a good living from their work that they have become role models for the local community. It is partly because Periyar and its wildlife are valuable to them that there has been no tiger **poaching** in the Park since 2000.

The future for Bengal tigers

The Bengal tiger is an incredible animal. It takes a unique place in the rich and complex natural world in Asia. That world is being changed by people on a larger scale than ever before.

Unfortunately, money is at the heart of the problem. Tiger **habitat** is shrinking because timber and cleared land are worth more money than forest. Tigers are being killed because their bodies can be sold at high prices. At the heart of the conservation of tigers then is one question: how do you make a live tiger worth more than a dead one, or a habitat with tigers in it worth more than one without them?

Of course, tigers should not need to have a value to be saved. Conservationists argue that we have no right to make any animal **extinct**. However, **ecotourism** is one example of how people can make money from the presence of tigers, not just a one-off payment for bones but regular income from tourists, year after year. They are therefore helping to conserve tigers too.

Trees, tigers and people

'You can only save tigers by saving forests. And if you save the forests, you also wind up saving the best, purest rivers and lakes ... And when you save your water sources, you save yourself!'
Bittu Sahgal, India Wildlife Protection, on the importance of tiger habitat to people.

However many tiger skins and bones are seized, it is poachers' attitudes that need to change for tigers really to be protected.

Although there are many dedicated conservation workers trying to save tigers and their habitats, many experts predict that all tigers could be extinct by 2020.

Tigers are a symbol of wildlife, but also a marker of where we have got to in human civilization. If we cannot save this magnificent creature, what chance is there for helping members of our own **species**, let alone the other species that tigers live among? Once tigers disappear from a stretch of forest, the will of governments and conservation groups to save that forest from the timber cutters often disappears also. Then whole **ecosystems** of animals and plants, which have developed over millions of years, disappear.

The Tiger State

In 1994 Madhya Pradesh was named 'The Tiger State' because of the number of tigers there, the number of **reserves** and the area of suitable tiger habitat. The state set up a Tiger Cell, combining the efforts of police and forest officers to seize **poached** items. Since then a possible model of tiger conservation has failed, because of corruption. Officials have allowed large areas of forest habitat to be destroyed. For example, there are around 10,000 sawmills, half of which are illegal, processing newly cut forest trees. Although a tiger count in 1997 claimed a rise in tiger numbers since the previous count, closer investigation suggests that numbers had in fact dropped, and that the original count was deliberately false.

How can you help?

The problems Bengal tigers face are so immense, it seems impossible that any individual can help them. However, if you want to help save tigers you can make a difference.

Learn more

You can read books, watch TV programmes and visit sites on the Internet. A good starting point might be your local library. How about learning about tigers as part of a class project?

Write a letter

People in government in India and other countries where Bengal tigers live make many decisions that affect tigers. For example, they make laws that control land use, and employ the police and **reserve wardens** who try to stop **poaching**. Governments in countries around the world can influence the use of and trade in traditional medicines containing tiger parts. Governments are more likely to make the right decisions for tigers if they receive letters from people concerned about them.

The more you know about Bengal tigers, the more you can tell others about their problems. These school children are learning about tigers and other animals in Corbett National Park, India.

There are various letter-writing **campaigns** you can contribute to. For example, the Save The Tiger Fund encourages letters to the prime minister of India. On their website they provide information to include in your letter and the address to send it to. You can also write your own letter and get others who agree with you to sign it. This is called a petition. People who sign it should also clearly write their name and where they are from.

> Just doing something, however small it may be, is a thousand times better than doing nothing.

Jenny's petition

Jenny Osgood of Cornwall, UK, learnt that there were at most 7000 tigers of all **subspecies** left on Earth. She felt so cross about this, and in particular about poaching to provide materials for traditional medicines, that she started a petition. She left copies of the petition in local shops and petrol stations. She also went with her family into her local town and asked people she met on the street to sign. Within ten weeks Jenny had collected 7000 signatures, one for every **endangered** tiger. She sent the petition to the UK Environmental Investigation Agency. They were so impressed they asked Jenny to take the petition herself to the Indian prime minister, Mr I.K. Gujral. Mr Gujral said his government was committed to saving the tiger.

Jenny's petition sparked off a children's campaign in India and worldwide coordinated by conservation groups including Tiger Link and WWF-India. There are already a quarter of a million signatures, and organizers are aiming for one million.

Donations

Many people help Bengal tigers by giving money. Some schools and individuals have 'adopted' a tiger. This means they pay money to help conserve a particular tiger, and receive information about it. You do not have to give much money. For example, you can donate subscriptions to *Cub* magazine to schoolchildren in India for around £1 a year. Their families usually cannot afford to buy them their own subscription. *Cub* is a great way for kids who live near tigers to learn more about them, and get involved locally in their conservation.

Glossary

ancestor earlier generations of living things. For example, your grandparents and great-grandparents are your ancestors.

breed produce babies

campaign organized activity to bring about change

carcass dead body of an animal

carnivore animal that eats other animals

colonizers people from one place who take over another place

customs officials who control the movement of goods between different countries

deciduous trees that lose all their leaves at particular times of year

descendant later generation. For example, you are a descendant of your grandparents.

development change aimed to improve land or habitat. Developers are the people who carry this out.

ecosystem community of co-existing organisms and their habitat

ecotourism a kind of tourism that aims to benefit habitats, wildlife and local people

endangered when a plant or animal is in danger of dying out

extinct when a species or subspecies has died out and no longer exists

food chain shows the order in which food energy is passed from plants to animals

genes parts of living cells that control how an organism looks and how it will survive, grow and change through its life

genus a classification grouping. In the genus *panthera*, the big cats, there are several species. In the cat family there are several genera.

glands small, specialized organs in various parts of the body

habitat place in the natural world where a particular organism lives

herbivore animal that eats plants

home range area within a habitat that an animal usually lives in

inbreeding when animals that are closely related breed together

irrigation   supplying water to the land and crops

livestock   animals kept for meat or milk, or to be sold

mammal   warm-blooded animal with hair that can feed its young with milk from its body

mark   sign left by an animal. For example, one animal leaves a scent mark to show other animals where its territory is.

monsoon   tropical rainy season in Asia

poaching   catching or killing an animal illegally

pollution   when part of the environment is poisoned or harmed by human activity

predator   animal that hunts and eats other animals

prey   animal that is hunted and eaten by another animal

reserve   area of protected land where animals and plants live safely

retina   thin layer at the back of the eye that reacts to light

scrub   dry habitat that often has thorny, low-growing plants

smuggle   transport something illegally, usually across borders of countries

species   type of animal that cannot breed successfully with any other type

stalk   closely follow prey in order to get near enough to catch it

subspecies   distinct type that can breed with other subspecies within a species. For example, Bengal tigers are a subspecies of tiger.

suckle   when a baby mammal drinks milk from its mother's body

suffocate   prevent from breathing

territory   particular area an animal claims and defends as its own

track   follow marks such as pugmarks (footprints) to locate an animal

tropical   area close to the equator where it is very hot

warden   person paid to guard a particular area, such as a reserve

water catchment area   area into which a lot of rainwater falls and collects in rivers and lakes

Conservation groups and websites

All these groups work to help conserve all five **subspecies** of tigers, including Bengal tigers. You can find out much more, including addresses and details about particular projects or fundraising, by visiting their websites.

WWF

www.panda.org
WWF (formerly known as the World Wildlife Fund) is a massive global organization committed to protecting the natural world. Tigers are one of their flagship species – recognizable animals that inspire conservation not only of tigers but also of their habitats. WWF has just launched a new conservation strategy and action plan to conserve different tiger habitats.

Save The Tiger Fund

offnature.roshd.ir/tiger/directory/savethetigerfund.htm
This giant US charity has spent more than $10 million on tiger conservation since 1995. It sponsors The Tiger Information Center's, Five Tigers website, which is one of the major places to find tiger information. It also provides links to other conservation organizations. You can use this site to find out details about writing protest letters.

IUCN – The World Conservation Union

lynx.uio.no/catfolk
The Cat Specialist Group is a team of scientists and wildlife managers from around the world with experience and knowledge of tigers. They are one group within IUCN. Their website has lots of details about all types of cats, including tigers.

TRAFFIC

www.traffic.org
TRAFFIC is an international trade control programme set up by WWF and IUCN. Their website details several initiatives to stop tiger **smuggling**.

21st Century Tiger

www.21stcenturytiger.org
A conservation partnership set up in 1997 between London Zoo and the charity Global Tiger Patrol. It funds projects as diverse as buying

jeeps and boots for **reserve wardens**, and training local people in conservation.

Project Tiger
www.envfor.nic.in
This Indian government site contains links to the Project Tiger reserves across India, and detailed information about the status of tigers in these reserves.

Other Indian conservation groups
There are many other dedicated tiger conservation groups in India. Here are just a few:
Tiger Trust
www.indiantiger.com/trust/index

Wildlife Protection Society of India
www.wpsi-india.org

The Wildlife Trust of India
www.wildlifetrustofindia.org

The Corbett Foundation
www.corbettfoundation.org

Books

Arjan Singh's Tiger Book, Billy Arjan Singh (Roli Books, 2001)
Natural World: Tiger – Habitats, Life Cycles, Food Chains, Threats,
   Valmik Thapar (Hodder Wayland, 1999)
The Secret Life of Tigers, Valmik Thapar
   (Oxford University Press India, 1999)
Tiger, Geoff Ward and Michael Nicholls
   (National Geographic Books, 1998)
Wild Tigers of Bandhavgarh, Iain Green (Tiger Books, 2002)

Videos

BBC Wildlife Special – Tiger – The Elusive Princess,
   narrated by David Attenborough (BBC, 1999)
Land of the Tiger, narrated by Valmik Thapar (BBC, 1998)

Index